TRUST
YOUR
JOURNEY

30 daily meditations for finding
joy, peace and purpose in life's challenges

Trust Your
Journey®

TRiLOGY
PERFORMANCE WORKS
publishing

If there's one lesson I've taken with me through my years in sports, business and government leadership, it's this: *life is what you make of it*. We can't always control the events of our lives. We can't control how people act toward us. We can't always control the challenges that life throws at us. But we can control how we respond to those events, people and challenges. Always.

I know firsthand that life can be tough. Life *will* be tough at times, I can promise you that. But you have to be tougher. You have to be stronger. And when you find yourself on your knees, exhausted and nearly defeated, you have to vow to yourself that you're going to get up again. And again. And again.

You have to "Trust Your Journey", believe in your journey, and believe in yourself.

This book provides inspiration and small steps we can make to remind ourselves that no matter where our life's journey takes us, we always have some degree of control over whether we let life wear us down and drain our joy, or stand tall and search for ways to find goodness and build maximum joy for ourselves and our companions in this world.

This book is easy to believe as I have watched Trust Your Journey's creator, Beth Brownlee, walk these lessons in her daily life. I am thankful that she would share with us these truths.

I pray that, with the help of this book, you discover light in your darkness, hope in your despair, and peace in the midst of your pain.

—**Gov. Judy Martz**, Former Governor of Montana
and 1964 Olympic Speed Skater

Having an enthusiastic outlook on life is the first step in seeing extraordinary changes. I've been inspired by Beth and her journey for nearly a decade, so I'm excited she's created *Trust Your Journey Meditations, Volume 1* to share her strength and wisdom with a wider audience. It's a must-have resource and an amazing gift for anyone looking to supercharge their happiness!

— **Devin Alexander**, NY Times Best Selling Author, Weight Loss Expert, Chef of NBC's "The Biggest Loser"

Trust Your Journey, Volume 1 is a delightful collection of timeless reminders of the good in life. They refresh and reset your mind, building trust in the journey that life is taking you on. This is a book to enjoy each day and in your own way. On your best days or on your worst days, take a moment to savor these pages.

When the realities of my husband's cancer and the difficulty of caregiving weighed me down, a moment with this book brought peace.

— **Helen Rockey**, CEO, See Kai Run

Meditation is something that benefits everyone, but a lot of people aren't sure where to start. *Trust Your Journey, Volume 1* provides great descriptions for the mindset and clear instructions for simple yet profound meditations. This is a wonderful, powerful book and tool for finding more peace and clarity in everyday life!

— **Doe Zantamata**, Inspirational Author

Do you wonder if your life is ever going to get better? Will this darkness last forever? Is life just an endless chain of meaningless days and sleepless nights?

If you're like me, you've struggled with the answers to these questions over and over and over.

Years ago, in the midst of my fight with cancer, I reached a point where I lacked the strength and will to live. I didn't see the point. I was, quite literally, sick and tired. Sick from cancer. Tired from chemotherapy. Not only was my hair falling out, I was beginning to lose my teeth as well. If I was going to feel like this for the rest of my life, what was the point in going on?

Then one day a friend gave me a small gift with three simple words—Trust Your Journey—inscribed on it. Reading these words ignited a fire of hope in my spirit. Life suddenly made sense, bringing comfort and peace to my soul. I believed and trusted that the awfulness of cancer would lead to good—someday, somehow. As my health returned, my life purpose became to inspire, comfort and encourage people all over the world in midst of their dark times. Over 10 years later, and still in remission, I continue to greet every day with the same enthusiasm as the first day I chose to embrace this life I've been given.

If you're at the end of your rope, it's my mission to give you words of hope and encouragement. What you're feeling right now doesn't have to define you.

You don't have to feel this way forever.

You can choose a new path, beginning today, with this book.

Over the next 30 days, you will read words of encouragement and take small steps toward a more positive outlook on your life. We call these Journey Steps—small daily steps that can lead to big changes if you commit yourself to this process.

Commit to reading every day. Commit to working on the Journey Steps. Commit to taking control of your attitude.

30 days. That's it. Can you do it? Of course you can! I have faith in you. Have faith in yourself.

Now, please, without delay, continue to Day One of your new adventure into the light…

Beth

Co-Founder
Trust Your Journey

You must do the things
you think you cannot do.
—*Eleanor Roosevelt*

Yes, You Can

Able:

Adjective

- having necessary power, skill, resources, or qualifications; qualified.
- having unusual or superior intelligence, skill, etc.
- showing talent, skill, or knowledge.
- legally empowered, qualified, or authorized.

Meditation

More times than not, the voice in your head is *not* your biggest cheerleader. That voice will remind you of all the things you cannot do, that you are unable to do.

It takes practice each day to flip our thoughts from "I can't" to "I can." But there's no better time than now to change that. You just need to turn up the volume of the voice of your heart.

When you listen to that positive, hopeful voice, your thoughts will shift from what you are unable to do to what you *are* able to do. Your view of life will change. Your view of those around you will change. Your view of *yourself* will change.

You *are* able. Yes, you *can* do this!

Blessing

May you hear the voice of your heart above all others and know you are able to handle whatever comes your way. Even if you don't have the experience and knowledge to get where you want to go, so what? You *do* have the strength and courage to take a fresh, new step in a positive direction. One step at a time, you *can* do it!

Today's Journey Step

Be conscious of your thoughts. Make them work for you and not against you. Encourage yourself. When your thoughts drift toward fear and doubt, intentionally tell youself, "Yes, I can!"

The most difficult thing is the decision to act, the rest is merely tenacity. The fears are paper tigers. You can do anything you decide to do. You can act to change and control your life; and the procedure, the process is its own reward.

—*Amelia Earhart*

Don't Just Sit There. Do Something!

Action:
Noun
- the process or state of acting or of being active.
- something done or performed; act; deed.
- an act that one consciously wills and that may be characterized by physical or mental activity.
- actions, habitual or usual acts; conduct.
- energetic activity.
- an exertion of power or force.
- effect or influence.

Meditation

How often do you find yourself sitting around thinking about volunteering for a good cause, cleaning up the garage or spending that much needed time with a friend? Or, maybe, it's just taking better care of yourself through rest, exercise and eating healthier. Don't just sit there with great intentions—take action. Do something! The ripple effect of your efforts will do more than just uplift your own spirit. Positive actions are contagious and provide encouragement to others to get up and do something as well. It's the "good goes around" principle. Whether you take the lead or join a group with a cause, one good action inspires others to do likewise, even coming back to you in unexpected new ways. Go put some good into this world. It needs you.

Blessing

May your good intentions turn into great actions. It's okay to start small. As someone once advised, *do for one what you wish you could do for everyone.* One step at a time, leave your mark!

Today's Journey Step

Take one action that positively impacts someone else. If no ideas come immediately to mind, call one of these local organizations and schedule a time to volunteer: food pantry, animal rescue shelter, or retirement community.

Security is mostly a superstition. It does not exist in nature, nor do the children of men as a whole experience it. Avoiding danger is no safer in the long run than outright exposure. Life is either a daring adventure or nothing.
—*Helen Keller*

Dare to Make Life an Adventure

Adventure:

Noun
- an exciting or very unusual experience.
- participation in exciting undertakings or enterprises.
- a bold, usually risky undertaking; hazardous action of uncertain outcome.
- a commercial or financial speculation of any kind; venture.
- peril; danger; risk.
- chance; fortune; luck.

Verb
- to risk or hazard.
- to take the chance of; dare.

Meditation

You are made for so much more than this life. You were made for adventure. To become fully alive you must step outside your comfort zone.

But what's adventure?

Adventure is the opposite of comfort and luxury. Those things are the enemies of joy. To fully experience life and all of its highs—and lows—you must be willing to take risks.

You must find your own balance between living joyfully and living foolishly. No one can find that balance but you. And you can't find that balance until you step out and search for it.

Blessing

May you accept this reality: you are wonderfully made, with the ability to do so much more than you can imagine today. May you begin to recognize this truth, starting right now.

Today's Journey Step

Do one thing today that makes you nervous. It doesn't have to an epic risk, like climbing Mount Everest. A baby step is still a step in the right direction.

Shared joy is a double joy;
shared sorrow is half a sorrow.
—*Swedish proverb*

Life Is Not a Solo Act

Alone:
Adjective
- separate, apart, or isolated from others.
- to the exclusion of all others or all else.

Adverb
- without aid or help.

Meditation

You may believe you are strong enough, capable enough to handle anything and everything life throws at you without anyone else. You may be strong. You may be capable. But humans are designed for relationships. We are social creatures. It's not just a spiritual principle, it's a scientific fact.

Odds are that someone else made the clothes you're wearing, the house or apartment building you live in, and the vehicle you ride in. From public utilities to grocery stores to electronic devices, we rely on others for the things and services necessary for life in this modern world.

Less obvious is your need for the emotional support that can only be provided by others. And only you can provide for them.

Blessing

May you grow to accept all the people in your life. Some will come. Some will go. Some will remain forever. Each of them has a lesson, albeit some of the lessons are greater than others. May each of these lessons make you stronger, wiser and more content.

Today's Journey Step

Reconnect with a friend or family member you haven't seen in a while. Schedule a time to meet them for lunch or dinner. It's time to catch up!

The purpose of life is to live it, to taste experience to the utmost, to reach out eagerly and without fear for newer and richer experience.
—*Eleanor Roosevelt*

Right Now Is the Best Time to Start Living

Begin:

Verb

- to proceed to perform the first or earliest part of some action; commence; start.
- to come into existence; arise; originate.

Meditation

Life is a one-way ticket with a limited number of sunrises and you don't want to miss any of them.

There's no better time than *now* to not just live but to *thrive*.

If you're physically capable, get outside. Go for a walk. Volunteer with a non-profit organization. Take a friend to lunch. Schedule a vacation. Visit a museum.

Are you unable to get outside? Bring people to you. Invite an old friend to come visit—have a meal delivered. Connect with old friends and new acquaintances through social media. Even better, call them on the phone!

Maybe it's time to develop new interests. Take a class at the community center. Sign up for an online course. Perhaps it's time to learn a new career. Don't let age or physical ability stop you. This is the Information Age—learning something new is just a few mouse clicks or screen taps away!

Blessing

Don't believe the negative self talk *lie* that the good life is all about sitting around doing nothing. On the contrary: the good life is about getting up, getting out, and getting going. You *can* live a better life. And you can begin *now*.

Today's Journey Step

What's one small thing that you've been meaning to do but have been putting off until another day? Guess what? Today's that day. Put down this book and *do it now!*

God gives every bird its food, but does not always drop it into the nest.
—*Danish proverb*

Change Requires Action

Change:

Verb

- to make the form, nature, content, future course, etc., of (something) different from what it is or from what it would be if left alone: to change one's name; to change one's opinion;
- to change the course of history.
- to transform or convert (usually followed by into)
- to become different
- to become altered or modified
- to become transformed or converted (usually followed by into).

Meditation

You are what you do. Not what you *say* you will do.

If something challenges you it can change you for the better. And some form of action must be taken in order for change to happen.

Maybe you just need a change of attitude toward someone or something.

Change might demand a physical movement such as exercising or eating differently if you want to be healthier.

One thing is certain—positive action leads to positive change. And positive change brings about positive results for life.

Blessing

May you find the strength to take action that can bring about positive change in your journey. You have that strength. If you search hard enough, you will find it. And when you do, the good changes can begin.

Today's Journey Step

What's one small change in your morning routine that can create a positive change in your life? Waking up ten minutes earlier to avoid chronic tardiness? 30 minutes earlier to exercise? Wise breakfast choices for a healthier start to your day? Something else? One small change can result in surprisingly big and positive changes. Try it!

Bad friends will prevent you
from having good friends.
—*Gabon proverb*

It's Time to Make a Break From Bad Company

Corrupt:

Adjective

- guilty of dishonest practices, as bribery; lacking integrity; crooked.
- debased in character; depraved; perverted; wicked; evil.
- made inferior by errors or alterations, as a text.
- infected; tainted.
- decayed; putrid.

Verb

- to destroy the integrity of; cause to be dishonest, disloyal, etc., especially by bribery.
- to lower morally; pervert.
- to alter (a language, text, etc.) for the worse; debase.
- to mar; spoil.
- to infect; taint.
- to make putrid or putrescent.

Meditation

Life is like a bus and you're the driver. Some people—your family and friends—will ride with you for a lifetime. Others will come and go through years. But, there will be a few who get on your bus with unhealthy baggage. When one opens up their bag and the negative contents spill out, stop the bus and let that person off. You owe it to yourself and your lifetime riders.

Blessing

May you always surround yourself with those who lift you up and have your back. May you have the strength to take a coffee break or lifetime break from anyone toxic in your life.

Today's Journey Step

Look closely today at the people on your bus. Now is the time to be brave enough to take a break from anyone that is bad company.

Life must be lived and curiosity kept alive.
One must never, for whatever reason,
turn his back on life.
— *Eleanor Roosevelt*

Stay Curious

Curious:

Adjective
- eager to learn or know; inquisitive.
- prying; meddlesome.
- arousing or exciting speculation, interest, or attention through being inexplicable or highly unusual; odd; strange.

Meditation

Curiosity is wonderful!

It keeps the journey exciting. It motivates us to look under every rock and behind every shut door for more—more knowledge, more information and more answers to the seemingly simple but oh-so-complex one-word question, "Why?"

When answers don't come quickly or easily, don't abandon your sense of curiosity. Some revelations take time. Others require us to seek harder and deeper than we're comfortable with. Be okay with the discomfort and patient with the timing—those are often the hallmarks of the best answers and eternal truths.

Keep exploring. Keep searching for new discoveries. Hidden behind the routine of every day are endless possibilities, unexpected answers, and unrevealed new journeys that propel us forward.

Get outside your comfort zone and never stop learning.

As Albert Einstein once said, "I have no special talents, I am only passionately curious."

Blessing

May you always, *always* stay curious toward life. May you be a lifelong student on your journey through this world.

Today's Journey Step

Seek out information on one subject you're curious about. Use the library, search the internet or ask a person. Start simple. Ready, set, go!

A rocky vineyard does not
need a prayer, but a pick axe.
—*Navajo proverb*

A Better Life Takes Effort

Effort:

Noun
- exertion of physical or mental power.
- an earnest or strenuous attempt.
- something done by exertion or hard work
- an achievement, as in literature or art.
- the amount of exertion expended for a specified purpose
- an organized community drive or achievement.
- Mechanics. the force or energy that is applied to a machine for the accomplishment of useful work.

Meditation

Often, we get in our own way in our efforts to create a better life without even realizing it.

We tell ourselves, *this is the way it will always be,* instead of making the effort, big or small, to seek a different path to an improved situation.

You are *never* stuck. By simply changing your thoughts, you can change your life. That bears repeating: *changing your thoughts can change your life!*

Do the best you can and never forget you don't have to be perfect. Just move forward. Inch by inch. Step by step. Hour by hour. Day by day.

Each day gives us the time we need to seek our greater good.

Blessing

May you know that God created you and you are enough. May you be motivated to make the effort—big or small—it takes to bring forth a better life and don't wait for someone else to magically fix your challenges.

Today's Journey Step

Take one small step today to improve one area of your life—just one. You are capable of great things so let's start with one.

If God can work through me,
he can work through anyone.
—*Francis of Assisi*

Yes, God Can Use a Person Like You

Endowed:
Verb
to furnish, as with some talent, faculty, or quality; equip.

Meditation

We tend to think of the Bible as a book filled with characters who are above average, who have talents and gifts that exceed our capacity. But read deeper and you'll discover that God tells his story through a group of misfits—murders, adulterers, liars, and hypocrites. If God didn't call sinners to do his work, whom would he call? You and I, we are all misfits. Even in this messed up dirty state we seem to find ourselves in, we are all perfectly suited to answer God's call whenever and wherever we are.

God needs you right here and now. You came into this world with special gifts that only you can give back to those around you. Your faith can move things, change things and create hope. Love God, love others as yourself, and pass it on. It's a simple formula to live by and an easy one to share with others.

Be open to wherever and whatever God has planned for you. God needs you because someone out there needs God.

Blessing

May you know each minute how much God loves you and needs you to be yourself. May you be kind with your words and frequent with your positive actions. Live life, trust God.

Today's Journey Step

Today share the gift of your smile with others. It's a simple yet powerful gesture that can change someone's day. Remind yourself at the top and bottom of every hour to smile.

Turn your face to the sun and
the shadows fall behind you.
—*Charlotte Whitton*

Focus on a Better Future, Not Your Past!

Future:
Noun
- time that is to be or come hereafter.
- something that will exist or happen in time to come.
- a condition, especially of success or failure, to come.

Adjective
- that is to be or come hereafter.
- pertaining to or connected with time to come.

Meditation

The past is where we should go for lessons and growth. It's where we should go for joy and fond memories. You will be taking daily trips to the past. It's normal and we all do it.

But, in your life journey, make sure you keep your hands on the wheel and your focus on the road ahead.

What lies in front of you is your precious future and all the great things that await. Leave your past where it needs to stay—in your rear view mirror.

Life isn't about going backwards, it's about today. It's about working toward a better tomorrow, a better you.

Blessing

May you find value in your past as you focus on this present moment. But may that focus be grounded in working toward a better future. May you keep your eyes on all that you can be from this day forward.

Today's Journey Step

What's one life-changing memory your thoughts often revisit? What lesson can you learn from that memory? How can that lesson lead toward a better future? Write that lesson on a sheet of paper and keep it in your pocket or wallet so you don't forget it!

How wonderful it is that nobody need wait a single moment before starting to improve the world.
—*Anne Frank*

Find Joy in Giving Joy.
Life Isn't All About You.

Give:

Verb
- to present voluntarily and without expecting compensation; bestow
- to grant (permission, opportunity, etc.) to someone
- to impart or communicate
- to set forth or show; present; offer
- to be warm and open in relationships with other persons.

Meditation

Giving and receiving are two sides of the same coin. While the receiver gets the gift, the giver gets the joy of positively impacting the life of someone else. This is more than just a spiritual theory—science confirms that a charitable spirit adds to our contentment with life.

In any one day there are gifts to be shared with endless people, places and events. You can give your time, talent, service and material assets. Or you can give something as simple as a hug.

Whatever you choose to do, just do something. Don't get caught up in yourself. Don't fear the perceptions of the receiver—the gift should be about them, not you. Don't worry about how to begin—just start small and grow from there. And don't wait—go find the joy in giving today.

Blessing

May you find the joy in giving each day. May your gift put a smile on your face as it lifts your heart and the hearts of others.

Today's Journey Step

Call your local school, museum, nonprofit organization or house of worship and ask how you can support them. Don't put it off. Put down this book and pick up your phone. It's time to find joy in giving.

A good memory is one that can remember the day's blessings and forget the day's troubles.
—*Irish Blessing*

Keep a "Goodness" Journal

Goodness:

Noun
- the state or quality of being good.
- moral excellence; virtue.
- kindly feeling; kindness; generosity.
- excellence of quality.
- the best part of anything; essence; strength.
- a euphemism for God.

Meditation

So many good things happen in our lives but for some reason, the bad things often dominate our thoughts and memories.

The best weapon for fighting those bad memories is your Goodness Journal. Grab a journal or a pad of paper and at the end of the day— or as they happen—write down the good things that happen, no matter how small. Even if it's just the smile of a friendly employee in your favorite restaurant. Or witnessing a young person help a physically challenged senior adult in their time of need. You can even paste in a printout of a humorous cartoon you saw on social media that brightened your day. It's your journal, be creative with it!

Every Sunday morning, spend 30 minutes reviewing your journal.

You will be *amazed* by the number of good things that life brings your way. That's a promise.

Blessing

May you always reach for an attitude of gratitude. May your written words remind you that the goodness does outweigh the negativity in life.

Today's Journey Step

Start a Goodness Journal today. Write down three things you are thankful for right now. It can be as simple as coffee in bed or hiking through a park. Do this every day this week and review it on Sunday morning.

Hurry, hurry has no blessings.
—*Swahili proverb*

Don't Be Held Captive to the Clock

Hurried:

Adjective

- moving or working rapidly, especially forced or required to hurry, as a person.
- characterized by or done with hurry; hasty.

Meditation

Wow, we live in a fast paced world these days constantly in a hurry to get from here to there, meeting deadlines, showing up for appointments and maximizing our days!

We dash around most of the time entranced in our routines and habits, held captive to a clock with an ever dwindling number of minutes and hours.

Why do we, exhaustingly, try to squeeze so much into a day?

It's what we know. It's what we see others doing on social media or hear they are doing at work on Monday morning.

There's nothing wrong with fulfilling your obligations and responsibilities. Just be sure you are not so busy that you forget about yourself, reducing the quality of your life.

Blessing

May you find precious moments each day to breathe in and breathe out, relax and just be. May you always know it's OK to take time for you and not to be hurried or rushed through any day.

Today's Journey Step

For the next three days, set aside 10 minutes to be conscious and bring awareness to the blessing of not being in a hurry. Give yourself a break!

There are two ways of spreading light:
to be the candle or the mirror that reflects it.
—*Edith Wharton*

You Are an Influence to Someone. Be a Positive One.

Influence:

Noun

- the capacity or power of persons or things to be a compelling force on or produce effects on the actions, behavior, opinions, etc., of others.
- the action or process of producing effects on the actions, behavior, opinions, etc., of another or others.
- a person or thing that exerts influence.

Meditation

How do you use your skills and experience to influence others in a positive way?

If you use your time in a way that you only focus on yourself, you will never be able to understand what others think and feel, and never develop empathy. If you are a bad influence you will lose respect, trust and love.

But when you influence others positively, you build a bridge of trust, love and kindness.

What you do affects others. The more good things you do, the more you uplift yourself and others. You develop empathy and compassion.

We all influence others but what's important is our intention. You can choose to be a positive influence. Or a negative one.

Choose wisely.

Blessing

May you always look for the chance to lift someone up. And never forget: like pebbles in a the sea of life, the ripple effect will be far reaching to others you may never meet.

Today's Journey Step

Today, when you see someone unhappy and not smiling, take the time to offer them a smile and show friendliness. Smiles are contagious.

Learning is not attained by chance,
it must be sought for with
ardor and diligence.
—*Abigail Adams*

Choose to Learn

Learn:
Verb
- to acquire knowledge of or skill in by study, instruction, or experience.
- to become informed of or acquainted with; ascertain
- to memorize.
- to gain (a habit, mannerism, etc.) by experience, exposure to example, or the like; acquire.
- (of a device or machine, especially a computer) to perform an analogue of human learning with artificial intelligence.

Meditation

When you finished school you probably tossed away your books, threw your hands in the air, and said "I am so glad my studying, test and project days are over!"

Little did you know that your most cherished learning days were just ahead of you.

You are a student all day, everyday for your entire life. Learning in the class of life.

The opportunity to learn something new each day is a divine gift. By choosing to learn you grow. And by growing, you make this world a better place.

Blessing

May you always be a student of life. Through the lessons you learn, may you discover the joy of sharing your experiences and discoveries with others.

Today's Journey Step

Lucubrate. That's an odd word, right? Go look up the definition, I'll wait here. Back? Congratulations, you've learned something new! Now, make it a habit. Choose to learn one new thing every day this week. This month. This year. It's not as hard as you've feared.

Never lose an opportunity of
seeing anything beautiful, for
beauty is God's handwriting.
—*Ralph Waldo Emerson*

God's Not Hard to Find.
Just Look Around.

Look:
Verb
- to turn one's eyes toward something or in some direction in order to see.
- to glance or gaze in a manner specified.
- to use one's sight or vision in seeking, searching, examining, watching, etc.
- to tend, as in bearing or significance.
- to appear or seem to the eye as specified.
- to appear or seem to the mind.
- to direct attention or consideration.

Meditation

So often we get caught up in our busy lives we forget to remember God is always present. Everywhere. All the time.

Choose to be a seeker always looking around for tokens of God's presence. You will discover the Divine in the smile of a stranger, the flight of a butterfly or your own breath.

Meditate on the miracle of a soft, white cloud in a blue sky, the fragile beauty of a rose, the expanse of the ocean or the majesty of a mountain range.

Don't complicate it. God's not hard to find and will never forsake or leave you. Put your trust in that.

Blessing

May you find comfort in knowing God is here, there and everywhere. May God's love surround you when are in the midst of the challenges of life.

Today's Journey Step

Make a list of three things that let you know God is present. Keep it simple. Then take a few seconds to be thankful for these reminders that God is always near.

Good people are good because
they come to wisdom through failure.
—*William Saroyan*

Making Mistakes
Makes You A Better Person

Mistake:
Noun
- an error in action, calculation, opinion, or judgment caused by poor reasoning, carelessness, insufficient knowledge, etc.
- a misunderstanding or misconception.

Meditation

On this awesome journey through life you are going to make mistakes.

Some mistakes will be big in your eyes.

Some will weigh heavy on your heart.

Others will be tiny enough for you to simply cast into the wind and move on.

Become a student of your missteps and allow them to teach you lessons that help you grow and become a better person.

Remember to grant forgiveness to yourself and others when mistakes are made. Forgiving yourself will not only ease your own mental burdens but show you the importance of forgiving others of their shortcomings.

Blessing

May you always have the strength to own your mistakes and be honest with yourself about them. A better YOU awaits just on the other side.

Today's Journey Step

Think back on a mistake you made in the past week. How could you have handled it differently? Reflect on it, learn from it, then let it go knowing you found your greater good in it. Repeat to yourself: *Never a failure, always a lesson.*

God is not a cosmic bellboy for whom
we can press a button to get things.
—*Harry Emerson Fosdick*

Sometimes you ask God for something
and you don't know what you're asking.
—*Mahalia Jackson*

Just Because You Ask, God Is Not Obligated to Grant Your Wish

Obligate:

Adjective
- morally or legally bound; obliged; constrained.
- necessary; essential.

Meditation

Wow, how many times have you asked, prayed and pleaded with God to answer a particular need in your life? You want it now!

Remember God's timing is full of faith, wisdom and love. However, it's also important to remember that the all-knowing Giver of life is not a magic genie, obligated to fulfill your every wish.

As Ruth Stafford Peale said, "There are three answers to prayer: yes, no, and wait a while. It must be recognized that no is an answer."

Nonetheless, always remember that God loves everyone as if they were the only one. Take comfort in knowing that the all-knowing, all-powerful force that created the Universe loves you—yes, you!—unconditionally. And, just like a loving human parent toward their children, God sometimes withholds our desires from us for our own good. Not to delight in our suffering but to protect us from even more tragic consequences.

When you are ready, He is ready. Ask away and know He hears you now. But never lose sight of God's perfect timing to answered and unanswered wishes.

Blessing

May you know that God hears all your prayers and with perfect timing provides the answers. May you have the insight to see that most unanswered prayers are in your best interest.

Today's Journey Step

Think back to your childhood. What was one thing you wanted from God so badly you'd have done anything to get it? But you didn't. And your life has been better because of that. What current wish could God be similarly withholding from you today?

When a man moves away from nature
his heart becomes hard.
—*Lakota proverb*

Day 20

Go Outside

Outdoors:

Adverb
out of doors; in the open air.

Noun
the world outside of or away from houses; open air.

Meditation

It's a documented fact that nature can help heal us from such things as anxiety and depression. A quick online search returns plenty of support for this premise.

Scientific research has found that a short walk outside can reduce negative thoughts in a matter of minutes.

Whether it's a star filled night or a garden by day, you will feel your spirit lift as soon as nature surrounds you.

Benefits of time spent in the outdoors include short-term memory improvement, renewed mental energy, reduced stress, reduced inflammation, and improved concentration and focus.

And you know the best part? It's absolutely free!

Give it a try. What do you have to lose? (*Here's a hint: nothing!*)

Blessing

May you feel the healing energy of nature. May the warmth of the sun or the simple song of a bird change your day.

Today's Journey Step

Get outside everyday this week, even if you have to bundle up or use an umbrella. It can be just five minutes or five hours. Take note of your senses. What do you hear? What do you smell? Breathe in and let it go.

The only person you should try to be better than is the person you were yesterday.
—*Unknown*

Don't Let Who You Were Define Who You Are Becoming

Past:

Noun
- the time gone by.
- the history of a person, nation, etc.
- what has existed or has happened at some earlier time.
- the events, phenomena, conditions, etc., that characterized an earlier historical period.
- an earlier period of a person's life, career, etc., that is thought to be of a shameful or embarrassing nature.

Meditation

There are things in your past you wish you could go back and change. Maybe it was something you said. Or something you did.

Holding on to a mistake from yesterday will only keep you from being all you're capable of becoming.

Sure, there are times we need to reach back to seek forgiveness or understanding. But don't stay there. Let it go in order to grow. Allow who you were to be a springboard to a better version of yourself.

Find gratitude for who you are but prioritize being mindful of who you are becoming.

Blessing

May you focus on the road in front of you rather than behind. May you grow into the "awesomeness" that you were meant to be in this lifetime.

Today's Journey Step

Write down three positive things you know or can do today that you did not know or do one year ago. Write down three things you want to know or do in the next 12 months and write down one step you can take to get there for each.

I never think of the future -
it comes soon enough.
—*Albert Einstein*

Live in the Present

Present:

Adjective
- being, existing, or occurring at this time or now; current.
- at this time; at hand; immediate.
- being with one or others or in the specified or understood place.
- being here.

Noun
- the present time.

Meditation

Meditate on this: you will pass through this life once and only once. Just one time!

Keep the short and temporary nature of life in mind for perspective about the value in *this* present moment—it's priceless! Right here. Right now. This moment will vanish forever.

Whatever you're doing *right now*—is it worth the value of a moment that will never, ever come again? Is this the *best* thing you can be doing with such a precious gift?

Worry is not worth your precious time. Nor is hurry. And certainly not reliving the past.

Choose wisely. The present is much more valuable than most of us can comprehend.

Blessing

May you embrace this moment as if it was more precious than gold or diamonds. Because it is. May you never waste one single second!

Today's Journey Step

Find a quiet place to pause for one minute and reflect on the present. Forget your to-do list. Forget worry, fear, guilt and sadness. Once this morning. Once this afternoon. And once this evening.

Action expresses priorities.
—Mahatma Ghandi

Examine Your Priorities

Priority:

Noun

- the right to precede others in order, rank, privilege, etc.; precedence.
- the right to take precedence in obtaining certain supplies, services, facilities, etc., especially during a shortage.
- something given special attention.

Meditation

Have you ever sat down and taken the time to truly examine the priorities in your life? What really matters, kind of matters, what to keep and what you could let go of?

You will always have your simple day to day "to do" list which includes groceries, cleaning the garage, etc.

But more importantly, *who* and *what* will get your attention in any given moment? Your free time is valuable and there never seems to be enough of it.

Our days are crazy busy between work and home, family and friends. You can't do it all *and* you don't want to find yourself the last item on your own priority list.

Carving out time to take an honest look at your priorities will be rewarding for you and others. Make the time, then make it happen.

Blessing

May your actions speak louder than your words on what truly matters. May you always keep yourself first and know that taking care of you will impact those around you.

Today's Journey Step

Today is the perfect day to take a close look at one thing that needs your special attention. What is it? Make sure that *one thing* is not being ignored and is properly placed on your priority list.

Start by doing what's necessary; then do what's possible; and suddenly you are doing the impossible.

—*Francis of Assisi*

Take Small Steps, Starting Now

Progress:
Noun
- a movement toward a goal or to a further or higher stage.
- developmental activity in science, technology, etc., especially with reference to the commercial opportunities created thereby or to the promotion of the material well-being of the public through the goods, techniques, or facilities created.
- advancement in general.
- growth or development; continuous improvement.
- the development of an individual or society in a direction considered more beneficial. than and superior to the previous level.
- Biology. increasing differentiation and perfection in the course of ontogeny or phylogeny.
- forward or onward movement.

Meditation

Is there something out there you have always wanted to do?

Maybe it was just to lose weight, give back to the homeless or take that adventure you've dreamed about for years.

There's no better time than now to take those small steps toward doing whatever that "something" is for you or others. Or even better, both!

Blessing

May you know that small steps are enough to keep you moving forward. May you have the confidence and strength to take those steps everyday starting today.

Today's Journey Step

Name one thing you've put off doing that you always wanted to do. It doesn't matter the size of the vision. Commit now to taking the first, small step that will move you closer to making that vision your reality.

Life is like a trumpet. If you don't put anything into it, you don't get anything out.

—*W.C. Handy*

Don't Just Sit There Waiting on Joy to Find You

Verb
- to strive to gain; seek to attain or accomplish (an end, object, purpose, etc.).
- to proceed in accordance with (a method, plan, etc.).
- to practice (an occupation, pastime, etc.).

Meditation

You must make a conscious decision to not wait on joy to find you.

Prince Charming is never going to ring your doorbell to take you to live happily ever after. Television will never take the place of real human relationships. A better job offer isn't going to arrive in the mail. Your physical challenges are not likely to simply disappear.

If you're waiting on joy to just show up, you're going to be waiting a long, long time. Go after joy. Get off the couch. Get out and go for it.

Visit a sick friend. Volunteer with a charity. Make something creative. And if you're physically incapable of going—call, write, or email someone. Or invite someone over.

Don't wait. Act!

Blessing

May you know that if you change your thoughts you change your world. May you realize that joy is within your grasp and choose to pursue it from this day forward.

Today's Journey Step

Go after one thing today. Joy can be found in simple ways. Carve out time for a friend, have an ice cream with a kid or schedule a minute of solitude for yourself.

We need to find God, and he cannot be found in noise and restlessness. God is the friend of silence. See how nature - trees, flowers, grass- grows in silence; see the stars, the moon and the sun, how they move in silence... We need silence to be able to touch souls.

—*Mother Teresa*

Day 26

Find a Quiet Place

Quiet:

Adjective
- making no noise or sound, especially no disturbing sound.
- free, or comparatively free, from noise.
- silent.
- restrained in speech, manner, etc.; saying little.
- free from disturbance or tumult; tranquil; peaceful.
- being at rest.
- refraining or free from activity, especially busy or vigorous activity.

Meditation

Most of us *make* time for stewing in our juices. Plenty of time. We don't plan it but it happens nonetheless.

But for some reason, we find it harder to make time to be quiet and still, to take a break from the chaos of life and our noisy, burdensome thoughts.

A quiet place is the cleansing ground for clearing out the clutter of our lives.

Find a place and a time that allows you to be alone without interruptions. It can be as simple as taking a long, warm shower or bath. Perhaps you can spend some time alone in a quiet library. Or perhaps having a sunrise breakfast alone with a hot beverage.

But wherever and whenever you find your quiet places, you must guard these places and times and habits greedily. Your life depends on it!

Blessing

May you find peace and hope by taking time to do less, not more. May you uncover the healing grace of quietness and gentle reflection.

Today's Journey Step

Take 15 minutes today and find a quiet place. Turn your devices off—you can be unreachable for 15 minutes. Don't solve the world's problems. Silence the voice in your head. Be calm. Breathe. Observe. Now make this a daily habit.

It is always the simple
that produces the marvelous.
—*Amelia Barr*

When Given the Choice, Choose Simple

Simple:
Adjective
- easy to understand, deal with, use, etc.
- not elaborate or artificial; plain.
- not ornate or luxurious; unadorned.
- unaffected; unassuming; modest.
- not complicated.

Meditation

What a blessing it is that we have choices. And you can rest assured there will be a multitude of them in any given day. With so many choices coming so fast, life can get overly complicated and agonizing.

How to get a grasp of it all?

There's an old idea called "Occam's Razor." In essence, this idea states that when you have a problem with multiple choices, the simpler one is usually better.

One trick for remembering this idea is to think of the word "KISS". That's an acronym for "Keep It Simple, Silly." Whenever possible, go with the simplest option. Simple is easy to understand. Simple brings order. Simple brings peace. Simple is better.

Don't be afraid to keep it short and simple.

Blessing

May you always be aware of the simple choices available to you each day. Simplicity is a gift. Be grateful for that.

Today's Journey Step

The next decision you have to make today—whether it be about work, health, relationships, or anything else— keep it simple and straightforward. Don't complicate it. KISS it!

Do not protect yourself by a fence,
but rather by your friends.
—*Czechoslovakian proverb*

Sticks in a bundle are unbreakable.
—*Bondei proverb*

In Difficult Times, Surround Yourself with Friends

Surround:
Verb
- to enclose on all sides; encompass.
- to form an enclosure round; encircle.

Meditation

There *will* be challenging times in your life. It's guaranteed.

That's the bad news.

But the good news is that there's strength in numbers, especially when those numbers include dear, true friends.

True friends always see the good in you, help you identify those traits and have a special way of lifting you up when you need it most.

They know when to just listen and they know when to talk.

Friends respect your "space" yet find perfect timing with a much needed hug, word of encouragement, helping hand, simple note of hope, or just sitting with you in silence.

They laugh with you and cry with you.

Who else would you want near you in difficult times? God's gift to you: your friends.

Blessing

May you have cherished friendships throughout your journey. May you be a friend to others in their difficult times along the way.

Today's Journey Step

Reach out to two dear friends this week with a text message, phone call or greeting card. Let them know how grateful you are that they are a part of your life. A simple "thank you" goes a long way.

Nobody, as long as he moves about
among the chaotic currents of life,
is without trouble.
—*Carl Jung*

You Are Not Alone in Your Trouble

Sympathy:

Noun

- harmony of or agreement in feeling, as between persons or on the part of one person with respect to another.
- the fact or power of sharing the feelings of another, especially in sorrow or trouble; fellow feeling, compassion, or commiseration.
- in psychology, a relationship between persons in which the condition of one induces a parallel or reciprocal condition in another.

Meditation

Troubling situations come and go in your life. In those times, we often think we are alone and the "only one."

In reality, there are many others who have traveled your path or are currently going through the same issues you are.

You are never alone in your trouble.

Talk about it and you will find there are others who will chime in with "me, too!" You will discover strength in sharing the journey with others.

After all—isn't traveling our journeys together what life is all about?

Blessing

There's strength in numbers. May you know you are never alone. Whether God, friends or a stranger—someone always has your back. May you see sympathy as a blessing, both to be given and received.

Today's Journey Step

Seek out people who have already climbed the mountain of trouble you're currently climbing. They might just have the wisdom you need for a better understanding of your journey.

It is common sense to take
a method and try it. If it fails,
admit it frankly and try another.
But above all, try something.
—*Franklin D. Roosevelt*

Take Action. Try Something

Try:
Verb
- to attempt to do or accomplish.
- to test the effect or result of (often followed by out).
- to endeavor to evaluate by experiment or experience.
- to test the quality, value, fitness, accuracy, etc., of.
- Law. to examine and determine judicially, as a cause; determine judicially the guilt or innocence of (a person).
- to put to a severe test; subject to strain, as of endurance, patience, affliction, or trouble; tax.
- to attempt to open (a door, window, etc.) in order to find out whether it is locked.

Verb
- to risk or hazard.
- to take the chance of; dare.

Meditation

What's that "thing" you have always wanted to do but never took the time to do it? There's no better time than now to step up, get out and try something new. If you are 69 and feel the need to ride the steepest roller coaster, then do it. Do you want to hike up Pike's Peak? Write a book? Learn photography? Get busy, take action and try something.

Blessing

May you have a lifetime of desires to try something new. Let your actions speak louder than your words.

Today's Journey Step

Today is the day to try something new. So what will it be? Time to shake it up and DO IT!